WALK WITH A T.H.U.G

Talented, Hard-working, Underrated, Gentleman

From FERGUSON

By

Lorenzo Davis Jr.

Copyright © 2021 by Lorenzo Davis Jr.

All rights reserved. No part of this publication may be reproduced, distributed, or transmitted in any form or by any means including photocopying, recording, or other mechanical methods, without prior written permission of the Publisher. For permission requests, write to the Publisher, addressed "Attention: Permissions," at the address below or email the Author directly.

ISBN: 978-1-7360697-5-2 (Paperback)
ISBN: 978-1-7360697-6-9 (eBook)

Cover Image by: Avenue K Designs

Printed in the United States of America

Robinson Anderson Publishing
2150 S. Central Expressway, Suite 200
McKinney, TX. 75070

This book is dedicated to my loving grandparents. I promise to continue our legacy. I love you Faye. See you on the other side Lula Mae, Arnold Sr., RoseMary and Roy Sr.

Table of Contents

Prologue	4
Ferguson Soldier	8
Street Poetry	9
St. Louis Stomping Ground	10
Fast Lane	12
Good Man, Bad Nigga	14
90s baby	16
Scars	17
Emotionally Scarred	18
Pressure Pressure	21
To Win it	22
A Fiend's Tale	24
Traumatized	26
King	28
Trapped	29
Energy	31
Mentally, Life is Hell	32

Visions	34
Love	35
My Queen	36
My Heart	37
Letter to My Prince	38
Next Chapter	40
Stuck Like Glue	41
King Talk	42
A Lou Night - A Short Story	43
About the Author	53

Prologue

Growing up a product of our environment they label us as low lives, needy, poor etc... Many of us are told that we won't make it to see the age of eighteen. In my city of Saint Louis, Missouri, unfortunately, most won't even make it to sixteen. With that in mind we choose to live the fast life, blow our money, and do everything we see our elders do because the lesson we are taught is, "you only live once." However, we aren't told that we can do better. We also are not told that it doesn't matter what tax bracket we are in or what our family members did before us. I believe that the righteous way is always the best way despite what I was told by those close to me at a young age. Through the years, I've done many things I'm not proud of but in my eyes doing wrong felt right because it was easy. Doing the right thing felt awkward to me because for so long I was doing the wrong things, living the street life which also including abusing drugs. However, I have come to learn that doing the right thing gives you peace of mind and you get better results.

Growing up a black man and loving rap/hip-hop music in my opinion, programs black men to use and sell drugs, be attracted to a certain type of female, party every night, stunt with material things, hate cops, rob, steal, kill, hate people and not be there like we should for our children. But in reality, we should do the opposite. We should try to increase our knowledge, save money instead of spending it, employ ourselves instead of selling drugs, live within our means instead of trying to impress others and better our community instead of destroying it.

We are quickly killing the generations after us by being a bad example. Kids are having babies at earlier ages; they are experimenting with drugs before they even reach high school and they're not even thinking about the repercussions of their actions. Furthermore, they want the easy way out without doing the work. But what they don't realize is that if you don't work hard for the things you want, they become of less value to you.

Many kids begin to run the streets during junior high school years, some start even earlier. We see the hustlers on the corners after school with fancy cars, pockets full of money, popularity, and power. What many kids don't see is that same hustler crying at night because of the people and things that they have lost. They don't see the police officer who harasses, extorts, robs and/or beats that hustler. Not all hustlers are bad. Many live this life because they feel like they don't have a choice due to their criminal records and not being able to get a job and some of them have criminal records for crimes they didn't even commit. But sadly, once that life is chosen, it's hard to get out. Not everyone is able to make it through the trauma and heartache, that's why only the strong survive. Females, cars, clothes, and money will never become extinct. Therefore, those things will always be available to obtain. Once you jump into the streets you automatically become a target; to police, your peers and to those who would rather take versus earn their way.

With those two groups of people watching you, it becomes a huge burden that you must carry for the rest of your "street" life. You can't move freely. You constantly have to look over your shoulder to make sure no one is out for you. Then, once you begin to accumulate a little money, you quickly become an addict. An addict is not just a person who needs drugs. An addict can be a person who needs money or needs the spotlight. Just like a drug, once you get that first taste, it's hard to give it up. Once you become addicted to the rush of the fast life, working for minimum wage will never satisfy you because, you can't do the same things you would be able to do getting street money. This lifestyle is highly addictive. If I had the power, I would classify it as a drug. Most people go into the streets with good intentions hoping to just make the money and support their family, but some others do it to prove a point or just to show how tough they are. In my opinion, that means nothing.

Going through life and dealing with an abundance of heart ache is too difficult for most people to handle. Often, people create their own heart ache, turning to the streets for an outlet. Yet, a person can only take so much pain before they give up and do what we call, "crash out." Crashing out can be committing a crime and not caring if you get caught or using a drug that you know is highly addicted which most times will cause you to commit the crime.

I watched many people go down this path, me being one of them. Turning to drugs to escape the harsh realities of life. Trying to numb the pain, not realizing that the drugs were just a temporary fix. Then, once the high faded, reality slaps you back in the face. The reality of life for some people gets heavy. The truth is sometimes the most difficult thing to handle. I understand why people commit suicide because, they can't handle life which is just an ongoing war that you must fight to survive.

I have experienced firsthand what these new age drugs will do to you and those people around you who care for you. I have done all the drugs that your favorite rappers lie to you about using. They tell you they take ridiculous amounts, knowing that if they took that much they would overdose and die. They leave it to the weak-minded people to experiment and kill themselves or just overdose. I took time to research every drug I ever did which included codeine, Percocet, Xanax, MDMA, Acid, Marijuana and Shrooms. These drugs put you in a trance leaving you in a fantasy world for a short period of time unless you constantly use them. Percocet binds to your opiate receptors in the central nervous system, which numbs the feeling of pain in your body. Abusing them numbs your mind to the pains of life which causes you to worry less or not even have remorse for things you do. Xanax in my opinion, is the worse because it affects chemicals in the brain. It slows down your brain activity. If you are in a panic or having an anxiety attack and pop a Xanax, your worries disappear. This is the reason I believe so many young people are killing each other. Many of them don't even realize they killed someone until they wake up the next morning trying to put the pieces together of what happened the night before because Xanax can also erase your memory once you go to sleep.

      We must do better, but change starts with us. Once people understand the benefits of being self-taught to heal, becomes easier. We have so many talented people but the box we're in, our voices are never heard. No one cares about our trauma because **WE** don't show we care. It's time for us to take a stand; lead by example and remember, we've all been there.

Ferguson Soldier

The news made our city look savage.

They didn't show when everyone came together, that part was classic.

Riots tore up our section, left so many with no work and strung out it, was tragic.

At the time I was stuck praying for a way out.

Unfortunately, being a product of my environment, I turned savage, my mental gave out.

Looting, shooting and getting maced became the way we lived daily.

Praying for better days but dark clouds surround; is there a better way? Maybe.

The streets turned up and I was a leader, but that struggle left us lost.

When the pharmacy got hit the team had drugs but for that lick, we paid the cost.

The city dried up fast and left so many with no more fight

within,

Forgive us for ours sins love heals all and together we win.

Street Poetry

Make money all day party hard all night.
The 365 days of a street hustler is nothing but stress.
Betrayal, robbery, shoot outs, police chases, funerals and court dates.

These are the oppressors of our struggles in the streets. The phase that majority of us face when we don't go to college and get thrown into the world to survive alone.

The world you know turns cold as you fight to find a road of your own. When you're grinding making money, people you thought were friends turn into envious foes.

Any moment your world can change for the best or the worst. Every minute of every day is a risk. Could you imagine the mental state of a person experiencing this?

St. Louis Stomping Ground

I made green in the valley that was my jump street.

Mean mug down Goodfellow, I kept the glock on my seat.

Shooting in Wohl's with the lost souls who had hoop dreams.

Racing down from Martin Luther King sipping that lean.

I got parked like a Natural Bridge my heart crumbling instantly.

Connecting the county to the city made so many envy me.

Meadowcrest was home base family tied 200 soldiers protected a T.H.U.G.

On the horseshoe they knew I'll pop like my OG, I had 33 on me like Illinois Trapping with Trav and Lee.

At 18 I was hood rich and labeled big homie.

At the time I felt all love didn't see that the streets were really phony.

When you supply the needs of everyone else, you feel lonely inside.

Your circle can be solid, but you got to watch the fake homies.

Giving selflessly expecting the love to be returned is a crash mission,

Losing and getting it back just to do it again, the definition of insanity.

Lost looking for love letting people in hoping you'd win,

But lurkers see you shine and come around to be fake friends,

To run off with hopes of hurting your pockets and never to be seen again.

That's the cry of a hood nigga living a life of sin.

Fast Lane

The fast life calls for quick decisions. You may have .5 seconds to make a life changing choice.

Many make the wrong choice because of the lack of knowledge they have for life.

Babies raising babies is the way the society has set up for them. That means a mom doesn't get a chance to reach her full potential as an adult before she has to teach a child the things she had just learned.

Grandmother's situation is usually worse, it's crazy the effects of this generational curse.

She had her daughter at 14 by her uncle but she can say nothing, so she has to live life in great mental pain.

The sons know their father but knowing the stress they put on the woman the man unconsciously removes himself from the household.

Chasing the fast life, the other generational curse that they have acquired. It keeps the father blinded and often times, the mother as well. It's a release, a breath of fresh air and is only temporary. The two results of the fast life are death and prison, but when times are good the thoughts of those two-go missing.

Generally, the fast life comes to an end either you come out on top, or you get broken down to build again. Some will never rebuild because they get stuck at a certain level and freeze up.

It would be amazing if more of the successors would lift them up.

Pay it forward and allow those that look up to you to use you. Make sure it's on your time and don't be afraid to take risks.

You have to study life only experience can teach you this.

Good Man, Bad Nigga

It's hard to walk straight when for years you displayed toxic traits

Once you get knee deep in the jungle you lose track of your true self and stop thinking straight

Bred by the best but hardheaded your third eye gets blinded

Because for everyone else's success you stress
Money makes you a King in the jungle what you say goes and you accept nothing less

Ego grows and you turn from a good man to a bad nigga

To the ones you love it means the world but to those that love you their lives become a living hell

Stress from the jungle you maneuver with ease
but when you come home that stress gets released

Unintentionally you lash out on the ones that truly care when all they want is for you to be there

Physically mentally and spiritually but it all becomes a blur

They want the same love you give to the jungle but your heads so big you forget how to be humble

You've fell for the trap of the government's strategically placed hell

You finally find a way out and lose everything you thought was yours going to jail

You start to gain but you feel you left your heart and always want to go back

Scared to adapt to the change because doing right now feels like a game

Trusting the good hurts because the bad scarred your soul

Real love feels fake
And fake love is like gold
Turning from King of the jungle to King of your family is a beautiful struggle
Turn your pain into passion the world needs your hustle.

90s baby

They 90s was real, raw and uncut.

We had great leaders in the struggle and to this day I feel the government set them up.

Tupac was bonafide and his words live on as if he were alive today.

Growing up in the struggle you gain respect when you lead the way. He was a Harriet Tubman of our time freeing us from the trapped mind.

The ghetto is set up to keep us under watch.

Control rules and if you don't pick up a book and learn your history, the world controls you.

Remember, you are somebody and your here for a reason. Find yourself and know your talents. Believe me the world needs them.

Scars

Where I'm from we tattooed our pain to represent what we did

Seen it all and done it all and we were just kids

Streets left us traumatized as teens growing to adults, cold hearted and scarred

Living past 18 we didn't think we'd make it this far

So many left us to the grave and to the prison yard

What we do after this? the OGs never mentioned that part

This level they never made it too so they couldn't navigate us through

Get money and save, but for what reason to buy a lawyer and live the rest of our lives like you

Blessed I was to have been led by greats,
I knew there was a better life but this street shit I had to escape.

Emotionally Scarred

Born into the world innocent and pure.

Loving everyone that shows love living with no worries or fear.

Exploring ways to live playing outside, boxing, excited to go to school just to see your peers.

Growing and learning yourself; building character finding your likes, dislikes and things you want to try.

Listening, learning and wondering how things work and how you can be like those before you.

Blinded by the troubles they faced protecting your innocence trying not to traumatize your brain.

Old enough to explore you, learn the hard way what they wanted to protect you from.

By then it's too late because your heads already been bumped.

Working to hide your pain keeping secrets from your protectors because you know right from wrong.

That wrong is so easy and painfully pleasing, you go back thinking you learned the way and can fix your mistakes.

You get trapped in the trap and get so far in it's no turning back. Forgetting that the power to overcome was already installed in you.

Making connections with your peers because they learned a different life, you jump in testing their waters not knowing how tainted their ways are from the ones who gave them order.

You strategize and use them for what their good at, putting yourself in danger.

Knowing the way to success, trying to incorporate their knowledge with yours will mentally damage you.

You get older and peer pressure takes over, every day you wake you don't want to go through sober.

The future becomes nonexistent, and you start living for the moment. Demon time in full affect when your true spirit is from heaven.

Trapping, robbing, killing and tricking slowly getting tricked out your natural position.

Leaving you stuck feeling you have to finish out this stage knowing you probably won't make it past.

You know it's levels to life but everything pulling you down how do you surpass

Time keeps ticking that shit be moving so fast.

High speed chases, funerals, court dates, shoot outs and heartbreaks. When will you ever catch a break?

You get 2 steps ahead and get knocked back 3.

You get tired of fighting and turn to codeine. Numb to everything emotionally scarred physically here but mentally gone.

Bouncing back comes from therapy learning to cope, but no one can focus on you because your innocence is gone, and they must provide and protect their own.
Who do you call on to pull you through? There's only one man I know that pulls you through. But you gotta believe and take the steps to overcome what you've been through.

This was all done before, so you will never be alone. Your body is rented your spirit has lived before.

Dig deep into yourself and look for guidance from the man above. You are him because he made you. Through him all things are possible walk that path greatness lives in you!

Pressure Pressure

I'm that young man that most need, I'm pressure pressure, yes indeed

I remind you of who you should be ambitious and ready for anything, I'm pressure pressure

You haven't lost your way you just lost the motivation I'm here to aid you back on the path to greatness, I'm pressure pressure,

When you thought your turn was up, but I come through and lift you up, I'm pressure pressure

If I win, you win and vice versa I'm not selfish I just know my worth, I'm pressure pressure

Some may say I'm arrogant I just know my purpose, I'm pressure pressure

I give opportunity, I plant seeds and give encouragement, I'm pressure pressure

So don't take me as a threat take me as the help the drive the push for you to bring back the best you, I'm just pressure pressure

That confidence boost when I step in the room, I'm pressure pressure
You had it in you the whole time you just needed someone to pull you through so in reality, *your* pressure pressure

Together we're pressure pressure, uplifting and encouraging without a shout of a doubt that's pressure pressure the way we rise in a drought.

To Win it

I never knew peace would come leaving the ones you love

I began to grow, and they stayed the same it sucks your stuck in your ways

Life plays on your mental and we do our best to lead with the heart

It was an uphill battle I guess it was time to stop falling down and having to restart

For some journeys to begin, some must end

You'll forever be in my heart in this game of life we must play to win.

A Fiend's Tale

Stuck in the mud I started drinking that shit

Whip the pack pussy pink feeling like my life was lit

Overdose after overdose waking up not remembering what I did
or who I was with

Turned out so many people to packs for years the guilt ate me up
I was unfit

Trapped not looking for a way out chasing the feeling I first felt
was the sad trick

After your tolerance gets high you find new ways to whip

Add a Xanax and a sleeping pill to the NyQuil sends you to space
really quick

Family hurt because you're a zombie and they raised you better
than that

Never be a user but my excuse was my back

The pain from a bullet that left the nervous system dead

Doctors said it's no way you'll get back your legs

Traumatized by those words, fuck life I quit,
then you feel the nerves twitch that's the sign of life

Workout go hard you're still in the game, but you have to fight

Mentally being drained dark clouds surround your brain

The most high sending you dreams of you walking again

A king fights through every battle life throws

What's life without pain no man knows.

Traumatized

Life's been rough lately. I lost everything I loved while being mentally set free.

I've carried the burden of many people while being numb to my own feelings. The feelings that always should come first.

The love of self. So many years being drawn to fake love knowing that it wasn't real. The love that was given as a child was materialistic not saying it was fake, but it left a hole in my chest and I didn't know how to feel.

Looking for the right kind of love that heals your heart sends you on many blank missions, following where faith takes you will always show the real.

What's meant for you will always be. At this moment I feel what's best for everyone is for me to not be here.

My legacy has been left I know my kids will never forget. Those that were close will always remember the effect I had on their hearts that genuine shit.

I have a healing spirit that's been golden from the start. So many have used and abused it my mind started falling apart. When would peace truly be mines and happiness for those around me get the chance to erupt.?

Give, give and give some more if I give you all of me what part of me do I get to adore? You having me without me having me is like a basketball game with no fans.

I put in this work in the gym to put on a show for you to make you happy, but when I step on the court to show what I've done for you there are no cheers to show you care.

I see you studying the work I put in maybe if I leave, you'll put what you learned to work. Instead of watching and criticizing as if you can do better don't just talk about it be about that will take you farther.

I feel like I've been running my whole life from family and friends but at the same time knowing I need them. The pain your family puts on you will drive any person insane.

I felt I should be the change the voice you need to get it together. I got my end together but helping those who don't help themselves mentally is a draining job.

We're here to heal each other but it feels like everyone is here to tear the next person apart. I cannot find peace living around this. When I know that there are places in the world where people live happily with no worries and less pain.

The only way for me to get that type of peace is to leave you alone my friend. May my love rest in you forever when it's tough times remember, be strong and hold on. Life is full of journeys find yourself and be true. You can make it if you believe, finishing starts with you.

King

I'm not African American, I'm a Black Native,

The descendent of a kidnapped African raped by America that produced a Nigga

I grew up a product of my environment, then I learned more about life and how to use this system

That put us less fortunate down and hid the secrets to success

I learned that life is really a game and when you're a pawn you don't notice, so I grinded until I became a King in chess

Putting my team together to orchestrate through life

Manipulating not to hurt but to lead them right

So, we can get what we came for easily and not have to deal with those who read our rights

The battle for a black native isn't easy but I got the recipe bring the ingredients and we can put them together and breeze through the higher levels of life.

Trapped

Jumped off the porch into the world feeling alone.

Got roughed up by the gang and start selling drugs wanting to get on.

The fast life is the fucking worse addiction.

It takes away the ones you love because they want something different.

All you see is live fast and die young, you don't you see the pain that comes with it because you blinded by green, but that green can only get you material things

Through quarantine I learned what love means. It's an energy that you feel when you are around real.

It's that hurt in the thought of losing something you thought was real

You can spend as much money as you want that don't make you real

Real is managing your time and giving love to self. Everything else falls in place from the vibrations of the earth itself

When you feel like it's all over you got to follow your heart that's the thing that makes you love from the start.

Follow the energy of that blood flow it will lead you to success.

Always remember there will be devils on the road it's part of the process

Stay true to you, stand for what's right and you will progress.

Don't get trapped there's more than one level to success.

Energy

I'm not your enemy,
I just love me and protect my energy.

I'm not your dope fiend,
This codeine helps me erase my memories.

I'm not your homeboy,
I was just a passenger in the car.

I'm not a celebrity but
I hold it down like a star.

I'm not your lover,
True love comes from within.

I am your plug,
Come get your daily dose of inspiration.

I am opportunity,
I can point you in the direction to win.

I am King,
I rule my kingdom you can learn if you pay attention.

I am the streets,
Look both ways before you cross me.

I am the struggle you can make it out of poverty.

Mentally, Life is Hell

Being a black man fighting against the system many of us fail.

We're taught to be strong then we become too strong for ourselves.

Which affects those close because emotionally we can't express how we feel.

Scarred, we become mentally and emotionally lost looking for love and we find it in the streets.

The big homie helps put money in your pocket then relive your stress teaching you violence.

Mentally the demons eat you up but again you can't show emotion, so you get deeper into beating yourself up.

Night sweats, fighting in your sleep using drugs to maintain mental peace.

You become an addict to the fast life killing, dealing and stealing,

Traumatizing the next generation because you don't grow even going to jail you learn no lesson.

You may find faith many become Muslim and see truth but when you come home you turn back to what you used to do,

Being a black man, many would not understand you have to separate from everyone create and stick to your own plan.

Bob Marley called it being a buffalo soldier because mentally you must set yourself free.

Life is a long journey, and you get what you make of it, so live free.

Visions

I see death around the corner.
As a man I've weathered so many storms
It only gets easier when I have you to hold in my arms.

Hearts been broken so many times all my feelings became numb,
Focusing on myself finally realizing how selfish I was.

Studying life because most of what we go through has already happened.

Seeking strength from my ancestors who fought until the war was done.

I've learned to never give up because that's when you lose.

We create the life we want to live and the battles we fight are the ones we choose.

The battle of love is painful and for you I'll fight time and time again.

In my eyes we're more than lovers everything we've been through made us best friends.

Love

Love is giving your all, risking it to have your heartbroken.

Love is a drug, and many are afraid of overdosing.

Love is pain, which is weakness leaving the body.

Love is just a word used to manipulate somebody.

Energy is the real feeling that makes you say the word freely.

So, when you tell someone, you love them it can have no real meaning.

Put the energy into it and in love they'll fall deeply.

My Queen

The way you hold it down Queen no one can compare.

When you walk your walk all the men stop, and they stare.

The way you rock that crown you kill every scene.

Your happiness is beautiful and deserves a wedding ring.

Big diamonds because what that pressure created is rare.

Strong, black, and independent, head held high walking with no fear.

Plus, you know to mold your man as long as he listens, he'll see.

How you stimulate his mind from all the devils that's deep.

Through all the trauma all the drama you never gave up.

Growing into you after every storm the sun shines again with new levels come new devils stay true.

My Heart

The air is clear
But you still have the blues.

Wondering if you'd feel the same if I wasn't next to you.

I created many storms I accept my truth.

Being lonely in this world hurts and it's something many go through.

I hope your heart heals and true happiness finds you.

If my heart must ache for it to happen that pain, I'll go through.

I can't stand the fact that I've hurt you,

Someday this will pass unconditionally, I'll always love you.

Letter to My Prince

My prince you're growing up and becoming a charming young man.

This world is dangerous, and people will see your kindness and mistake it for weakness.

My advice to you is stay humble, know yourself and be firm in your decisions.

I believe to be a successful black man you must be a T.H.U.G a Talented, Hardworking, Underrated, Gentleman.

I'm going to impart this knowledge in your mind as a child so when you grow older you can look back and see how this helped you survive.

First and foremost, show respect, make sure you set a good first impression.

If they show signs of disrespect that person has served your life no purpose, dismiss their presence.

No conversation you run your world you must protect your energy.

Secondly stick to the principles and morals that you feel help you grow mentally.

Believe in love, truth, peace, freedom and justice. Those are 5 basic principles of life that helped me grow into the man I am today.

Peace be the journey; the vibrations of the earth will lead your way.

Rule #3 always listen to understand don't listen to respond. Listening to respond you may miss a key point and it could cause the conversation to change completely.

Have patience ask questions don't assume or answer without thinking.

Rule #4 when taking a person seriously look them in their eyes. Looking into their eyes will give you a better connection with the soul you're communicating with.

Rule #5 fear no man alive. You are a God be true to your feelings those that are meant to grow with you will follow you.

Next Chapter

Chapters close, feelings get exposed.

Dreams become nightmares
But your still alive like a freshly planted rose.

Discipline is life, having control is rare.

Follow the leader, put in work stay down 10 toes.

Have no fear, we are all human we shit, sleep and stare.

Have faith, hold your head high the grind takes time every second counts have no fear wait for your time.

Stuck Like Glue

Devils tried to tear us down
Make us break apart.

But in your love, I drowned
You stayed down from the start.

From day one I knew what I wanted
I was built on structure and strong families.

The process be so hard when your mental is damaged, living it out is the only way of understanding.

No one explained this part of the game to me,

There was no handbook, no rules.

You stayed true with your mind, body and soul,

You're love to me is worth more than gold.

This love is a marathon it's full of long strolls,

Finding you, finding me, we build and be bold.

No one can stop us now, we defeated the odds.

To the next level we grow
As long as we have faith there's no limit to how far we can go.

King Talk

They only see the shine because we hide the pain.

The journey of life hurts you lose people only the bonafide remain.

2020, the year of vision opened our eyes to the game.

It unveiled the scars from this life of pain
And opened our eyes to let the tears of alcohol pour.

Healing the scars that man has created from the risk taken wanting to grow.

Moving forward the past hurt is understood and going backwards is no more.

I'll Always choose you and by law of attraction you'll enjoy life for sure.

A Lou Night – A Short Story

In Saint Louis, Missouri the night is the time that street hustlers a.k.a. dope boys clock in for work. Being such a large city, the competition is large and the street life is a dirty game. Each side of town has their main suppliers, but it's a free city, so hustlers travel to any part of town where money calls. The Northside hustlers make moves on the west, Southsiders make moves on the north and the county is fair game for anyone. The Lou is flooded with drugs. Users range from the age of fourteen all the way up to eighty.

What I Remember...

If you needed to unwind and escape from your reality, Tai-Tai and Biggz were the west side dope boys. They were feared by many, hated by few, and the love they got from the city outweighed any negative vibes. Throughout the day they made runs, picking up money from fronts that were given out the day before. They were good guys and had street codes they stuck by which were: respect, loyalty and honesty. If you associated with these two in any way, you for sure wouldn't burn any bridges. If you got a front, your debt was to be paid the next day. They rarely gave anyone credit for longer than 24 hours. If you couldn't pay when you were supposed to, they would part ways and not deal with you again, but if it was big money, you better be prepared for one of their young goons to come pay you a visit.

However, fiends weren't the only ones to get fronted, other hustlers were fronted with money too. From these fronts, they would collect more drugs. Supply and demand was the name of the game. These hustlers had so many was considered a downgrade and also an insult to their lives.

Tai-Tai the oldest of the duo was a certified wheelman; he was always the driver. Tai-Tai was a real go-getter. He loved to put people he trusted in positions to make money. Biggz kept the most clientele. He had the charm, "slick talk," and he knew how to negotiate. He could sell sand to a man in the desert.

Tai-Tai was about 5'10" with the heart of a lion. Biggz on the other hand was a big guy about 6'2" and 200 pounds of all muscle. They grew up together and treated each other like brothers. They started out hustling together after they met during a fight where some guy was getting the best of Biggz and at the time, little Tai-Tai jumped in to help him out. They haven't left each other's side since.

When five o'clock rolled around, the two stayed close to their neighborhood because their night shift was starting. The working class would clock out of their jobs by three in the afternoon and make their runs so they could hopefully be home unwinding by sundown.

Xanax, Percocet's, Marijuana and Heroin were the top drugs in the Lou and if people didn't get their fix every day, they would have withdrawals. On this day, there was no call at exactly five o'clock which was highly unusual, but the two hustlers paid it no mind as they sat in their neighborhood supplying their friends, family and customers who would walk to them.

The customers in their neighborhood didn't have much money at times, Tai-Tai and Biggz knew that, but they still stuck around because they loved to make their loved ones happy, plus they didn't want them to get tricked by money hungry goons. The first and the fifteenth of the month is when they made good money in the hood. Those were they times the government checks hit and everybody was "hood rich." The hood was live a few days after the first and fifteenth until, all the money was spent, then, it was back to starving and struggling, but those little moments of happiness lived in their hearts the entire month. There was a lot of love in the hood and the residents looked out for each other.

Uncle Spade, the neighborhood mechanic and one of the oldest dope fiends was very close to the guys. He would wash cars, cut grass, do maintenance on the homes, fix and wash Tai-Tai's car to get funds for his Heroin fix. Tai-Tai primarily paid him with his drug choice of the day. Uncle Spade known as the life of the hood kept everyone in good spirits and knew the neighborhood like the back of his hand. He would let people stay in his house which was paid for because it was handed down from his great-grandmother. Sometimes, he charged a fee to stay but most times if you kicked him down a drink, a blunt or some nose candy, he would appreciate that. Uncle Spade was a dope fiend and very proud of it. He didn't want to fix up or change his ways for anyone. Tai-Tai and Biggz made sure Uncle Spade had what he needed always.

Old man Nate was a loyal customer as well. He would spend six to eight hundred dollars a week just to get his fix. His drug of choice was Heroin. Uncle Nate was a functioning drug addict. He worked Monday thru Friday sometimes even on the weekends. When it was his time to unwind, Uncle Nate did just that. He would turn off his phone and enjoy his high. Nate respected the guy's hustle even though he didn't know them very well. However, Tai-Tai and Biggz knew him well. When five-thirty rolled around, they knew that they would be getting a call from their loyal customer for a guaranteed two-hundred dollars.

On the way to Uncle Nate the phone rang again, another southside customer who had one hundred-fifty dollars to spend. That's one-hundred seventy-five dollars apiece in less than thirty minutes. Nate loves to give knowledge so, every time he saw the two guys, he felt the need to drop some of his wisdom. Tai-Tai and Biggz respected that and even with money waiting on them they took a few minutes of their time to listen.

The night went on and more money was made. The two traveled through the city for hours hitting every part of town north, south, east and back west. Riding threw the downtown area of the Lou was beautiful especially with the sun setting around eight o'clock. The sun would set right behind the Gateway Arch over the Mississippi River. It was now eight-thirty and business started to slow up a bit, so they headed back to the neighborhood to count their earnings, put the money and most of the goods they had left away.

In their neighborhood, they could pretty much hide their goods anywhere but, they had a couple of girls they grew up with and trusted to keep their belongings safe. Thirty-two hundred dollars was the total amount of money they had accumulated in just five hours. The two would not travel if a person was spending under one-hundred dollars. That was more than the average person would make in one month.

Now, back in their comfort zone, it was time for Tai-Tai and Biggz to unwind after a long evening of easy work. It was late so, the two went to the liquor store to fill their cooler with beers and load up on cigars to roll up their marijuana. At the liquor store, they ran into Uncle Spade; that was his usual hangout. He would wait around the store just drinking his beers when no one was chilling at his house which was the party spot.

"Hey Unc, we kicking it at yo' spot tonight?" Biggs questioned.

"Nephew that's a question you aren't got to ask, mi casa es su casa." Uncle Spade replied.

They went back to the block to share with their family and friends. Tai-Tai turned up the radio in his car and let the base from his fifteen-inch subwoofers rattle the street.

Everyone was out dancing, celebrating and enjoying the night. The phone rang, it was Mr. Nate calling again. Biggz picked up the phone to see what he wanted as it was unusual for him to call twice in one day. It was even more unusual for him to call this late in the night.

"Yo Biggz! My neighbor here wants to meet up with you guys. Sorry for the late call but I'm not sharing. I have to make my package stretch a couple days. Can you come meet up with him? He's cool and a good working man."

Biggz and Tai-Tai were now under the influence and usually didn't make runs when they were under the influence as to avoid any encounters with the police. Any encounter with the boys in blue would often be a bad one in the Lou, especially with the reputation that the two had in the streets. Since it was Mr. Nate who was such a good customer, they made an exception. The hustlers went to their stash spot, hoped in the car and headed south. Mr. Nate's friend was a younger man named Damien who did electrical work. He was an ex-con who Tai-Tai knew from school. He was grimy back then, so they were hesitant to serve him, but since Mr. Nate vouched for him, they made the transaction.

"Long time no see Damien. How has things been for you, bruh? I haven't heard anything about you since you went to jail after school." Tai-Tai stated.

"Yeah, I was locked down for five years but, my head is on straight now. I'm just trying to make an honest living."

"That's good to hear, said Tai-Tai. I hope that works out for you. Keep ya head up."

Tai-Tai and Biggz went on their way.

Leaving Mr. Nate's house with an unexpected five-hundred dollars and already buzzed, Biggz told Tai-Tai he was feeling too good to go back to the neighborhood, so he suggested they head over to the eastside and visit the strip clubs. Feeling himself as well, Tai-Tai headed east toward the fleet of strip clubs in small town Brooklyn, Illinois. The eastside is what they call that area and any given night something bad was bound to happen.

This was the hustler hangout, if you were getting money, this was the place to be, but if you had beef you were bound to find your enemy or even just a drunk hater mugging you ready to attack.

Tai-Tai and Biggz weren't in their right minds and they usually didn't travel to the east alone, but they were fearless and just wanted to have a good time tonight. The Pink Slip strip club was a place that the two visited frequently. They were known by the DJs, dancers, bartenders, security and even the owner. They walked in and automatically got escorted to a V.I.P booth where they would get to tip the girls and get exclusive dances from their favorites. Two girls approached the guys in their private booth ready to make some money. They were mesmerizing and one stood out the most; her name was Sparkles. She was a tall dark-skinned beauty, with a sexy stance, pretty eyes, and the body of a goddess. She entered the club a few minutes after the guys and she had her eyes on the money. Kandi was her good friend they had met a few months back at the club and have been tight ever since. Kandi was a real ghetto girl with a classy side, she was average height with a nice body, very aggressive but sexy at the same time. The guys blew the five-hundred dollars they made moments after arriving at the club, but it was party money for them, so they didn't care. The girls loved every minute of it and didn't want to walk away.

"Yawl sure know how to treat a lady," Kandi yelled over the loud music in the club.

"Yeah, we spoil hood rats' yawl only good for a night anyways," Biggz said as the liquor was taking over him.

After about three hours in the guy's private booth, the girls had enough money to end their night on a good note. Sparkles and Kandi went to the dressing room to shower and get changed. Sparkles made a call to her man,

"Babe, these two ballers in here tonight and they are giving me and my girl all attention and making it rain." Simply, letting him know that she was coming home with more money than she would normally make.

"Well don't come home until their pockets are empty, I'm chilling right now, so you know what to do call me when you're ready to leave."

"Do you know the guy's names?"

"One is Tai-Tai and I think Biggz is the other one but, I got you babe I'm gonna try to leave with them. I will call when I get to their place to let you know everything is ok."

"Ok love be safe and stay alert. I don't want to resolve any problems tonight" the boyfriend added as he hung up the phone.

Sparkles did whatever her man wanted. He was an ex-hustler and was under supervision from the state, so he let Sparkles be the breadwinner in their household. Kandi was feeling as if it was a good idea to get with the two after the club. She felt that Tai-Tai and Biggz were handsome so what could they lose?

After about an hour later, the two stumbled out of the club laughing and slapping fives with everyone. Kandi and Sparkles followed behind them not ready to end the night just yet. The fellas took the dancers back to the hood and Uncle Spades house was still lit up at two in the morning. Kandi was familiar with the neighborhood pointing out Uncle Spade's house and wanted to visit her Uncle even though she was drunk and had sex on her mind. They knew for sure she was a hood rat after spotting Uncle Spade out of all people. Tai-Tai was with it, he just wanted to have a good time and he knew Uncle Spade was the right person to end the night around.

Kandi and Uncle Spade sat on the porch and got reacquainted. He wasn't her real uncle but, in the hood, most people called the older men uncle and older women auntie. She had known him for some time because her dad used to hang out with him back in the day.

Biggz, Tai-Tai and Sparkles were in the basement listening to music, smoking and talking. They were drunk and letting the dancer know all about their business. They told her how they made money and how much they usually made per day. Sparkles was drunk but, still sat there taking the information in. She started getting bored and wanted more fun, so she started pouring shots for the guys to drink. She had the guys out of their minds and ready to do whatever she wanted. They figured they were getting some good sex that night. Little did they know Sparkles was money hungry and had a man she truly loved waiting for her. Sparkles kept going to the bathroom making Tai-Tai and Biggz kind of disgusted with her. They felt as if she were throwing up or had a bad bladder. However, what she was doing was making calls to her man letting him know she was ok and that he should come pick her up before the sun rose.

Four a.m. rolled around everyone started winding down. The guys figured they would stay at Uncle Spades for the night. Uncle Spade high and drunk as could be, was not ready to sleep his high away. He sat on the porch playing music with his head nodding in the cool breeze. He looked up and a man was coming out of the alley with a black mask, black clothes and latex gloves on. The man ran up to Uncle Spade's porch with a .40 caliber handgun. He demanded Uncle Spade not to talk. Ordering Spade to lead him to where his girl Sparkles was, Uncle Spade had no choice but to show the man the way. The robber slapped Biggz with the handgun. He then slapped Tai-Tai. Kandi heard the ruckus and woke up screaming. She got pistol whipped. Sparkles woke up in kind of a shock, but then, she noticed it was her man. He was coming for all their money.

Sparkles and her man did this often. She had been planning the robbery the entire night. She knew where the money and drugs were because Tai-Tai and Biggz told it all. Biggz tried to talk his way out.

"SHUT UP" The man yelled and cocked his .40 Cal. Then put it to Biggz's head. The robber demanded the money from their pockets. Which they were empty after spending everything on the girls. He snatched Kandi's bag.

Biggz gave the man an address after noticing that Sparkles was in on the scheme. "That's not over here babe that address is on the Northside." "He told me they keep everything in the hood." Sparkles blurted.

Boom! Biggz was smacked again. "You must want to die stupid muthafucka."

Tai-Tai picked up on his voice. DAMIEN! Tai-Tai yelled right before Damien put a bullet in his head. Damien panicked, then two more shots went off into Biggz's chest.

Bloom! Boom! Off went two more into poor Uncle Spade. Kandi tried to run, Boom! Off went a bullet into her back. Sparkles started to scream, "Babe no killing, you tryna go back to jail?" "He recognized me; I-I mean what you expect? You wanna die too? If not, I suggest you bring yo' ass on!"

Damien left with his girl Sparkles and no money as he headed towards the address Biggz gave to her. "You think I killed them babe?" "Yeah, their dead for sure!" Sparkles exclaimed.

Everybody is connected in this city some way somehow, but it's every man for himself. No, one is to be trusted, man or woman. If Tai-Tai and Biggz would have stuck with their first minds and never went to meet Mr. Nate, none of this would have happened.

Life in the streets is a dangerous gamble. You never know what you might get into in A Lou Night.

About the Author

Lorenzo Davis Jr., a Saint Louis Missouri native by way of Ferguson, has experienced many hardships; many being self-inflicted. He has overcome drug addiction, the judicial system, street hustling, gang violence, childhood trauma and mental health issues. Most young black men are taught not to open up, show emotion and to always be tough which are good lessons, however, we are just as human as anyone else. Being able to express yourself however you see fit is a beautiful thing. So yes, stay strong, but be transparent, show emotion through your work and always provide and protect. Being a young entrepreneur and community leader has lifted Lorenzo up to new heights mentally and physically. In sharing these poems of his mental transition from the streets to corporate America, he hopes to inspire his elders and lead generation Z by example.

"We don't always choose the hand we're dealt but we do decide how we play it"

------**King Zo**

www.ingramcontent.com/pod-product-compliance
Lightning Source LLC
Chambersburg PA
CBHW072209100526
44589CB00015B/2452